ᯔᮓ ᬛR

ᯅᮤ ᬛ᮲ ᮰ᮓ

HMONG ALPHABET

ᮔᮓ ᯔᮢ

Level 1

ᯅᮘ ᬛ᮲ ᬛ

HMONG
MULTIMEDIA

Hmong Alphabet: Level 1
Copyright © 2014 Hmong Multimedia
hmongmultimedia@gmail.com

𖬒𖬰𖬧 𖬖𖬰𖬤 𖬗𖬱𖬞𖬟 𖬗𖬰𖬬 𖬖𖬰𖬮 𖬒𖬰𖬮 𖬉𖬰𖬛𖬰 𖬗𖬰𖬝𖬟 𖬒𖬰𖬜 𖬒𖬰𖬧 𖬜

Author:Chia Koua Vang
Editor: Ka Lee Yang

ꠜꠢ ꠔꠢ

ᤏᤠᤴᤛ

ᤏᤠᤴᤛ ᤘᤠᤶᤫᤧᤧ | ᤏᤠᤴᤛ ᤏᤗᤠᤵᤫᤧ

ᤘ   ᤑ

ᤗ   ᤑᤠ

ᤖ   ᤕᤠ

ᤗ   ᤕ

ᤗ   ᤗᤠ

ᤗ   ᤗ

ᤗ   ᤕ

ᤗ   ᤗ

ᤗ   ᤗ

ᤗ   ᤕ

ᤗ   ᤗ

1.   ... 13 ..., ... 13 ...

2.   ... 26 ...

3.   ... 20 ...

4.   ... 5 ...

[illegible]

[illegible]

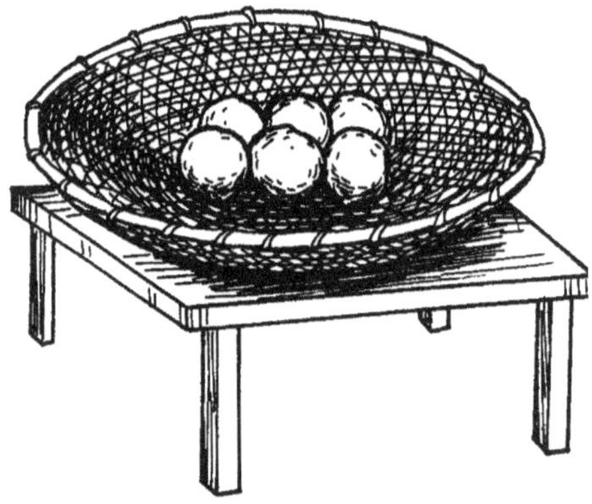

[illegible]

[illegible]

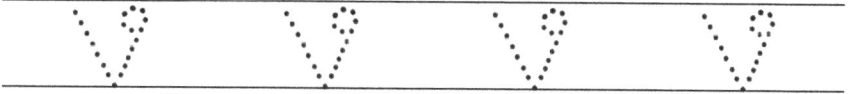

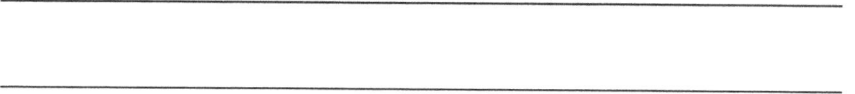

ໜ ່ A	ໜ ຕໜ	ໜ ຣ ໜ ໜ

7

ᤗ

ᤗ = ᤗᤠᤴᤢ

ᤗᤣᤕ, ᤐᤠᤰᤗ, ᤗᤠᤠ, ᤗᤢᤏ

ꓨꓯꓼ ꓧꓲꓬꓸꓣ ꓮꓲꓮ̈

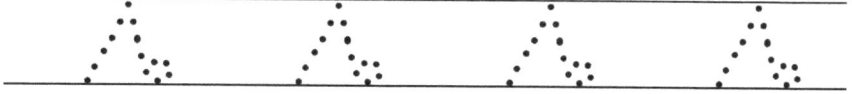

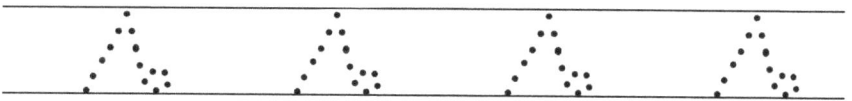

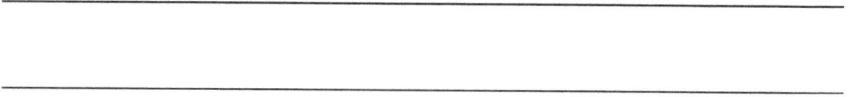

ꓧꓹꓥꓸꓮ̆	ꓧꓳꓵ̈	ꓧꓯꓹꓣꓸꓧꓹꓮ

9

ᨕᨙ

ᨕᨙ = ᨕᨙᨗ

ᨕᨙᨗ ᨕᨗᨖ, ᨕᨙᨕᨗᨖ, ᨕᨗᨖᨙ, ᨕᨙᨕᨗᨖ

ꓥꓳꓯ | ꓥ ꓳꓵ | ꓥꓯꓣ ꓴꓵ

ᄭ

ᄭ = ᄭᄭᄭ
ᄭᄭ, ᄭᄭᄭ, ᄭᄭᄭ, ᄭᄭᄭ

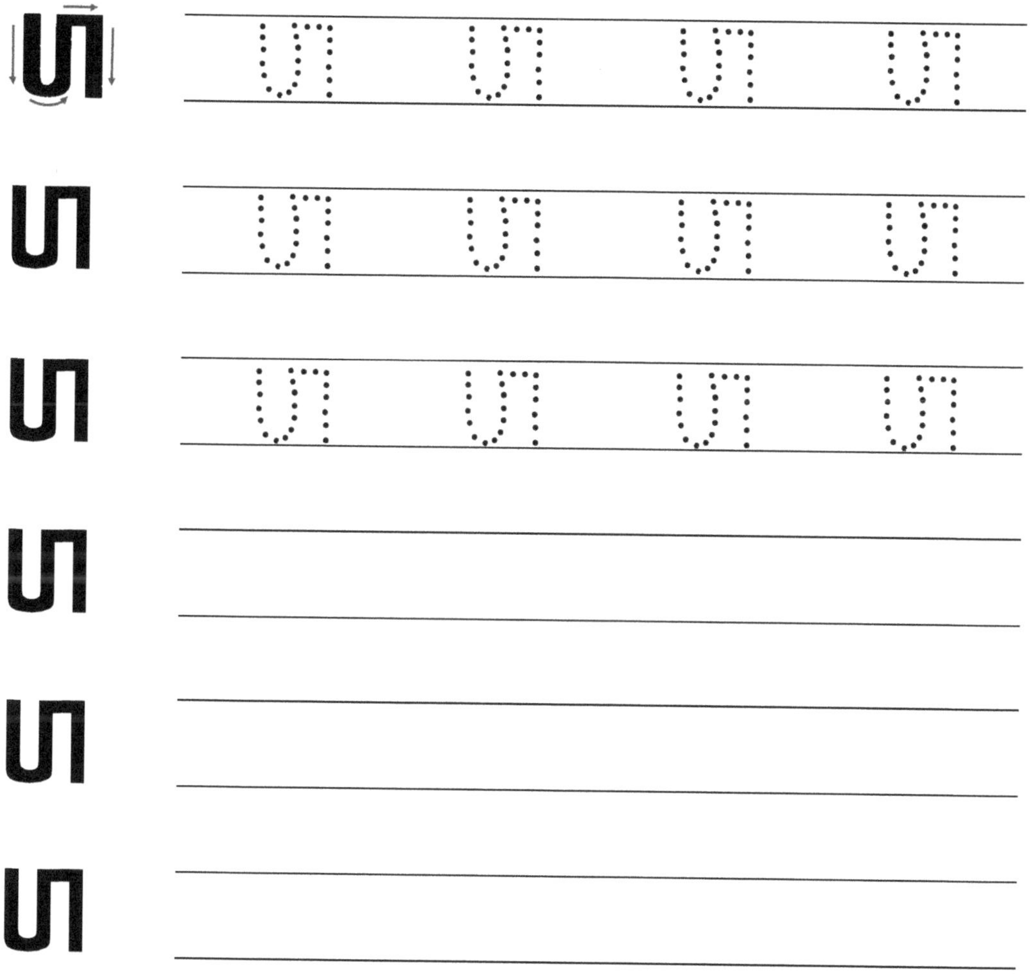

ປ

ປ = ປ໋

ຫຫປ໋, ຫໍຫໍປໍ, ປໍຫໍຜ໋

ຍ

ຍ ຍ ຍ ຍ

ຍ ຍ ຍ ຍ

ຍ ຍ ຍ ຍ

ຍ

ຍ

ຍ

ໝວດ	ໝໍ້ຍ	ໝໍ່ລິຂະ

H

H = Hᨯ᩠ᩞ

Hᨯ᩠ᩞ ᨅᨯ᩠ᩞ, Hᨯ᩠ᩞ ᨶᨅ᩠᩵, Hᨯ᩠ᩞ ᨲᨯ᩠ᩞ, Hᨯ᩠ᩞ ᨬᩘᨯ᩠ᩞ

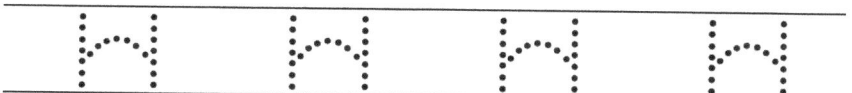

ĦꝟꙆ	Ħꙭꙮ	ĦꙆꙞꙪ

17

ᑌᗯ ᐯᕦ

18

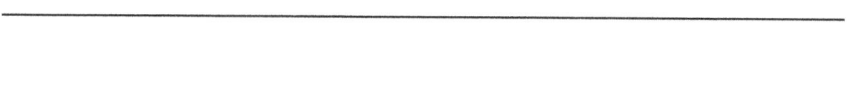

ᨣ

ᨣ = ᨣᩮᩢᩥᨠ

ᩅ᩠ᨿᨾᩣᨠᩢ᩠ᨣ, ᩅ᩠ᨿᨷᨠᨣ

ᒥ   ᒥ   ᒥ   ᒥ

ᒥ   ᒥ   ᒥ   ᒥ

ᒥ   ᒥ   ᒥ   ᒥ

ﻩﻭﯩ	ﻩﯗﯲ	ﻩﯸ R ﯺﻼ

Ꞙ

Ꞙ ꞊ Ꞙ ꞗ

ꞗꞘ, Ꞙꞗ, ꞗꞘꞗꞘ, Ꞙꞗ

ฑ ฑ ฑ ฑ

ฑ ฑ ฑ ฑ

ฑ ฑ ฑ ฑ

ษ ฝ Ẫ	ษ ผฺ ฒ	ษ ฝ ฿ ผ ฝ

ဂ

ဂ = ဂ့ၢၥ

ဂ့ၢဂ, ၵၡဂ, ၵၡ့ိဂ, ဂ႙ၵဆၵ

ក

ក ក ក ក

ក ក ក ក

ក ក ក ក

ម ៣ ៣	ម ៣ ៣	ម ៣ ៣ ៣

ᨸ

ᨸ = ᨷ, ᨷᩢ᩠ᨷᩯ

ᨳᩯ᩠ᨷᨸ, ᨸᩣ᩠ᨠ, ᨠᩣᩯ᩠ᨷᨸ, ᨷ ᨷᩢ᩠ᨷᩯ

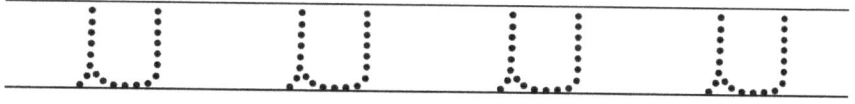

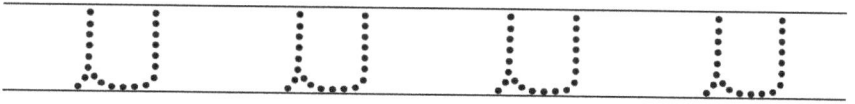

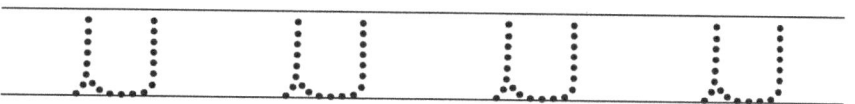

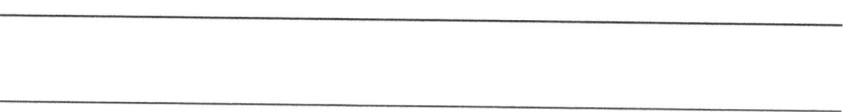

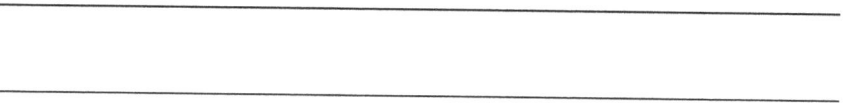

ꤜꤘꤢꤢ	ꤜꤢ꤬꤮	ꤜꤟꤛꤤꤘꤢꤟ

ᥓ

ᥓ = ᥓᥬK

ᥓᥝᥧ, ᥓᥓK, ᥓᥣK, ᥓᥴᥞ

ᩉ᩠ᩅᩢᩣ	ᩉᩮᩬ᩠ᩣ	ᩉᩢᩁ᩠ᩅᩢᩢ

ᥖ

ᥖ = ᥖᥱ

ᥖᥱ ᥝᥕ, ᥖᥱ ᥣᥕ, ᥖᥱ ᥐᥣᥲ

ᤳᤢ   ᤳᤢ   ᤳᤢ   ᤳᤢ   ᤳᤢ   ᤳᤢ

| ᤜᤴᤣᤠᤵ᤺ | ᤜᤜ᤺ᤢ᤺ | ᤜᤜᤪᤴᤠᤴᤣ |

ᤜᤠᤕ ᤎᤨᤵ

ᤁ

ᤁ = ᤁᤡᤘᤠᤵ

ᤁᤜ, ᤁᤖᤢᤵ, ᤋᤡᤰ ᤕᤠᤵ ᤁ

ᤀ

ᤀ

ᤀ

ᤀ

ᤀ

ᤀ

ᤜ ᤗᤣ ᤀᤠ	ᤜ ᤙ ᤐ	ᤜ ᤀᤠ R ᤏᤣ

ᨴ

ᨴ = ᨷᩥᩅ᩶ᩉᩣᨠᨴ

ᨧᩥᨠ ᩅ᩵ᩁᨴ, ᨴᩂᨠ, ᨣᨼᨻᨸᨣ

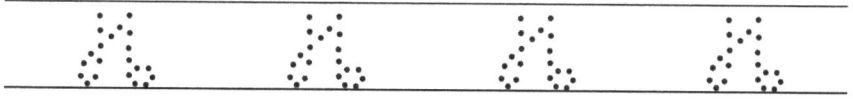

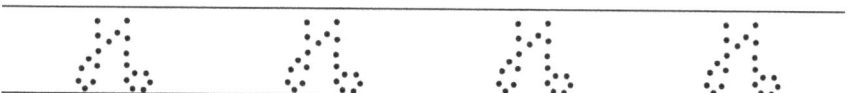

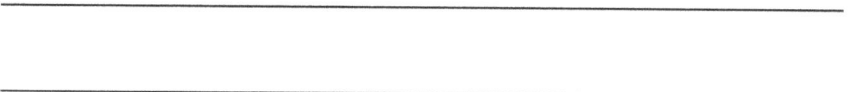

ꨨꨯ ꨄ	ꨨ ꨯ ꨮ	ꨨ ꨣꨯ ꨮ

ᩆ

ᩆ = ᩆᩃᩘ

ᨠᩫᩢᩆ, ᨠᩴᨿᩉᩅᩆ, ᩆᩴᩉᩁ, ᨶᩁᩆ

ຕ   ຕ   ຕ   ຕ   ຕ

ห ว ้	ห ต ໍ	ห ໍ R ห ้

ᨠ

ᨠ = ᨠᩡᩴ᩠ᨿ ᨿᩢᩴ᩠,
ᨠᩡᩴ᩠ᨿ ᩅ᩠ᨷ, ᨽ᩠ᨷ ᩇ᩠ᨠ ᩡᩴ᩠ᨿ ᩅ᩠ᨷ

ꀕꑾ

ꀕ

ꀂ

ꀂ

ꀲ

ꀲ

ꍬꃀꑾ	ꍬꀱꑾ	ꍬꀧꀜꑾꊿ

ꨟ

ꨟ = ꨟꨘꨪ

ꨓꨪꨟ, ꨟꨯꨱꨚ, ꨟꨮꨲꨇꨓꨮꨰꨵ

41

ᦠᦱ

ᦠᦱ = ᦜᦱ ᦶᦜ ᦠᦱ
ᦶᦜᧅ ᦠᦱ, ᦂᦽᦵᦣ ᦶᦜᧅ ᦹᧄ ᦠᦱ

ហ្វា

ហ្វា   ហ្វា   ហ្វា   ហ្វា

ហ្វា   ហ្វា   ហ្វា   ហ្វា

ហ្វា   ហ្វា   ហ្វា   ហ្វា

ហ្វា

ហ្វា

ហ្វា

| ห วา | ห อำ | ห ารหำ |

ᩅ

ᩅ = ᩅᩡᩅ ᨶ∀ᩅ

ᩈᩣᩴᨷᩮᩅ, ᩈᩣᩴᨷᩢᩪᩅ

ຜ

ຜ

ຜ

ຜ

ຜ

ຜ

H ν Ă	H ω̇ ω̈	H ʌ̇ Ṙ ω̇ ʌ̇

ဃ၁

ဃ = ဎ်Rဃ

ႇ̀ဃ, ကဒ̆ဎ်Rဃဟဲ

ແ

ແ ແ ແ ແ

ແ ແ ແ ແ

ແ ແ ແ ແ

ແ

ແ

ແ

H ່ ່ ໍ	H ໄ ໄ	H ໃ R ໃ ໍ

ᤕ

ᤕ = ᤐᤡᤱᤕ

ᤐᤡᤱᤕ ᤏᤡᤣ ᤏᤢᤰ, ᤐᤡᤱᤕ ᤐᤢ᤻ᤔᤢ᤻

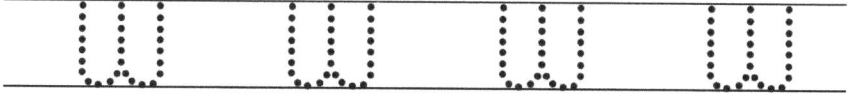

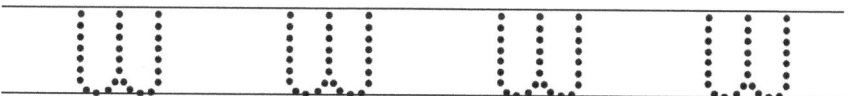

ꤜꤛꤢ꤬	ꤜꤢꤚꤢ꤬	ꤜꤢ꤮ꤤꤢ꤬ꤜꤛꤢ꤬

ຫ

ຫ = ຫບໍ

ຫບົກ, ຫຸR, ຫໍຍ, ຫຶໜໍ

ຫ

ຫົວ | ຫມູ | ຫາຣົບຫາ

ᨻ

ᨻ = ᨻᩬᨠ

ᨻᩊ, ᨻᨲᩣᩊᩥ�, ᨻᩖᨿ, ᨠᩬᩴᨻ

ภาษาเขมรเริ่มต้น

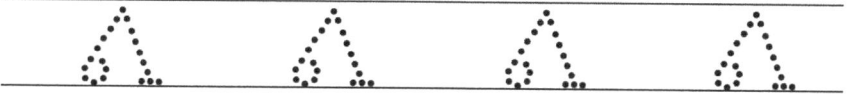

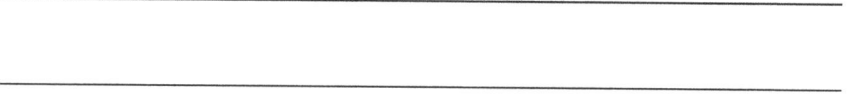

ผนวา	ผออื	ผารผผ

53

ᦢ

ᦢ = ᦢ ᦶᦙ

ᦅᦳᧄᦢ, ᦢᦱᦘ, ᦢᦳᧆᦱ, ᦢᧈᦞ

| ห่v̆ | หผื̆ | หÅ̇Rผ̇ |

ภ

ภ = ภอ

ภ ลิ่ม, ภ ซ้ำ, ภ ซก, ภ อิ่ม

ꤊ

ꤊ ꤊ

ꤊ ꤊ

ꤊ ꤊ

ꤊ ꤊ

ꤊ ꤊ

ꤜꤟꤢꤩꤛꤢꤩ	ꤜꤢ꤬ꤞꤢ꤬	ꤜꤢꤪꤖꤟꤢꤩR ꤜꤢꤨꤑꤢꤩ

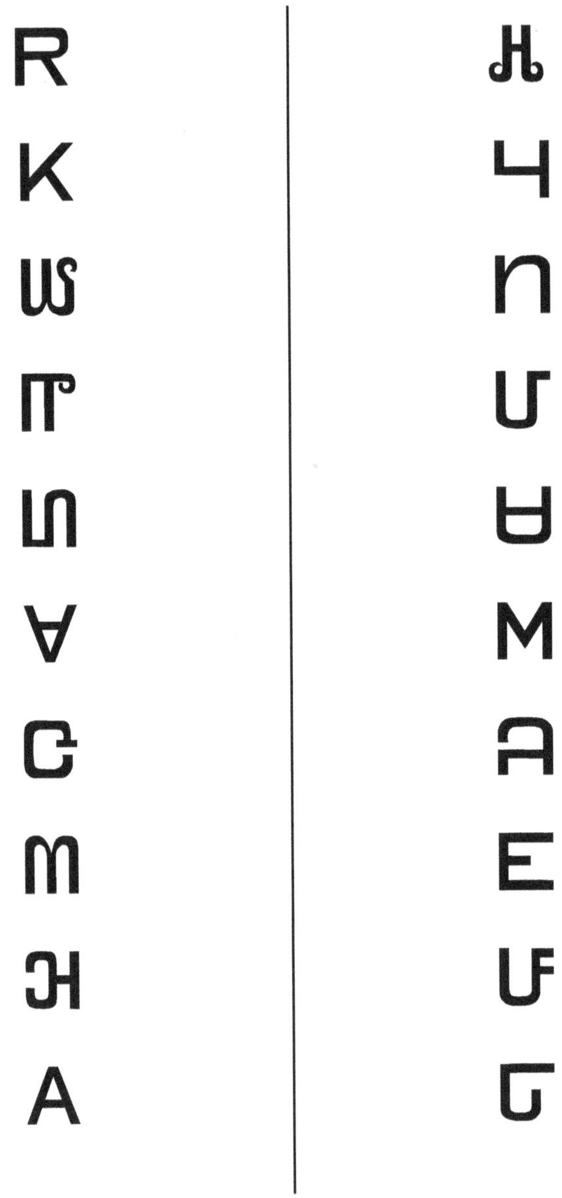

ᗰᨠ

R

K

ᗯ

ᨦ

ᐯ

C

ᨴ

Ⴆ

A

Ⴒ

ᅚ

ᑌ

Ⴌ

M

E

Ⴆ

ᒐ

ก ฆ งก ตกฺ

งก ตกฺ ขฺ ยก ฆ

1. ยก ฆ ฺ ฺ ก R 20 กฺ, ยก ฆ ขฺ
ยก ฺ, ยก ตฺ ขฺ ยก ฺR ฺ. ฆ ฺ, ลฺ
ตA ฺ ยก ตฺ ฺ ฺ ฺ ฺก ลฺ ฺR ฺ ยก
ฆ ฺ งฺ. ฆ ฺ ฺ ฺ, ลฺ ตA ฺ กฺ
ตฺ ฺ ฺ, ฺR ฺก ฺ กฺ ฆ ก งฺ ก
ฺ ฺฆ กฺ ตฺ ฺ ฺก ฺ ฺ ฺ ก ฺR.
ฺ ฺก ฺ ฺ ฺ ฺ กฺ ฺ ฺ ขฺ ฺ ก R
ฺก ฺ ฺ ขฺ ฺ ฆ ฺ. ลฺ กฺ ฺ ฺ ฺ
ขฺ ฺ ฺ ฺ ฺ, ฺ ขฺ ฺ ฺ งฺ.

59

ບໂກ

R

R = ﻼR

∩R, ﬃR, ﺟR, ﬅR, ﬀR

R R R R R

R R R R R

R R R R R

R

R

R

ﬞﬠﬡﬢ	ﬣﬤﬥﬦ	ﬧﬨ R ﬩ﬞﬠ

K

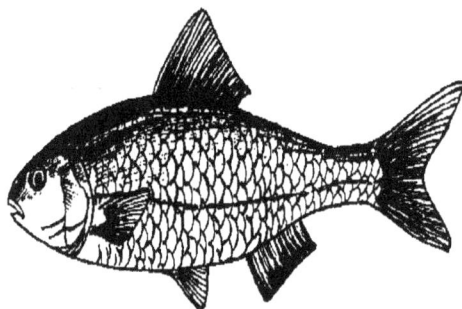

$$K = \bar{H}K$$

ЛК, U̇K, ÅK, VK, ᅲK

K K K K K

K K K K K

K K K K K

K

K

K

ꤜꤢꤛꤢꤛ | ꤜꤢꤢꤛ | ꤜ ꤢꤛ R ꤢꤛ

ພຣ

ພ = ວິພ

ຫພຣ, ວິພ, ກົພຣ, ວົພ, ຕາພ

ꦮ

ꦮ	ꦮ	ꦮ	ꦮ

ꦮ

ꦮ	ꦮ	ꦮ	ꦮ

ꦮ

ꦮ	ꦮ	ꦮ	ꦮ

ꦮ

ꦮ

ꦮ

ꦩꦥꦲ	ꦩꦗꦲ	ꦩꦲꦫꦲꦲ

ᒋᒄ

ᒋᒄ = ᑌᒊᒋᒄ

ᗽᒋᒄ, ᗯᒋᒄ, ᕲᒋᒄ, ᕳᒋᒄ, ᒐᒋᒄ, ᑎᒋᒄ

ꤜꤢ᷊ꤢ᷄	ꤜꤢ᷊ꤢ᷄	ꤜꤢ᷊ꤢꤛꤢ᷄ꤛꤢ

ຕກ

ກ = ທກ

ມກ, ວກ ຄກ, ຮກ ໝກ, ຫກຯ

ꨟꨳꨮ	ꨟꨮꨳ	ꨟꨓꨮꨟ

A

Ⱥ

Ɐ

Ɐ

Ɐ

Ɐ

Ɐ

ᕼᐯᐱ̆	ᕼᏯᏯ̆	ᕼᐱᏒᏯᏯ

ᥴ

ᥴ = ᥢᥴ

ᖴᥴ, ᥩᥴ, ᥙᥴ, ᥬᥴ, ᥝᥴ, ᥧᥴ

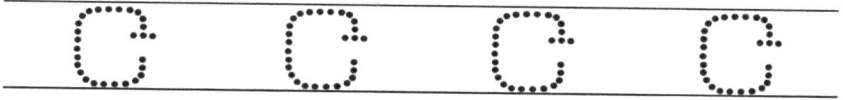

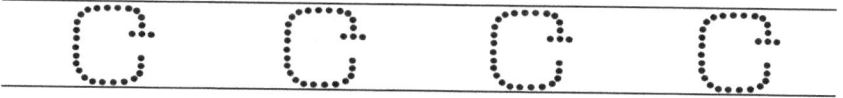

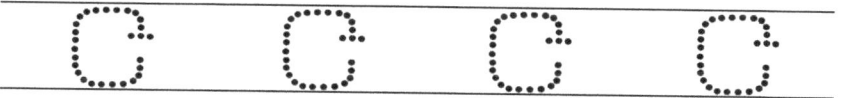

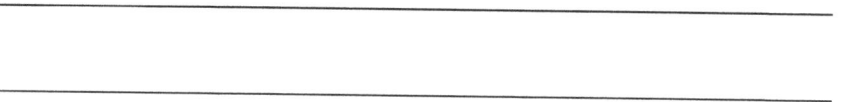

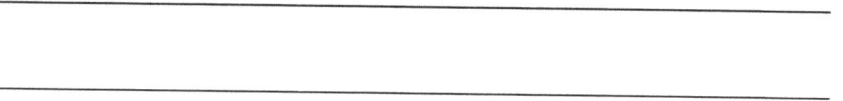

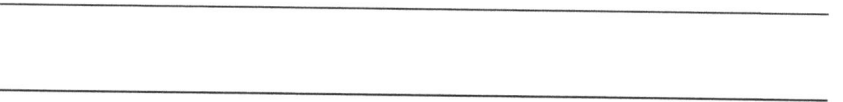

ᠮᠥᠩ᠎ᠠ	ᠮᠣᠳᠣ	ᠮᠠᠷᠢᠶ᠎ᠠ

៣

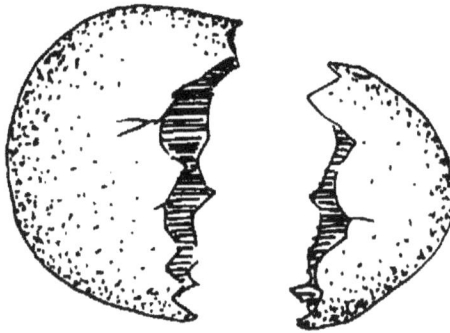

$$៣ = ២៣$$

អ៊ុក, កំក, ២៣ អ៊ុ រ៉ុ, អ៊ុក ម៉ុក

ᱮᱢᱮᱴ ᱵᱟᱱᱟᱹᱨ ᱧᱩᱢ

ᱢ

75

ຂ

ຂ = ຂົວ

ໂຂ, ເຂ, ແຂ, ໍຂ, ບຂ

ꦗ

ꦗ ꦗ ꦗ ꦗ

ꦗ ꦗ ꦗ ꦗ

ꦗ ꦗ ꦗ ꦗ

ꦲꦮꦴ	ꦲꦏ�꧀	ꦲꦭꦫꦠꦤ꧀

A

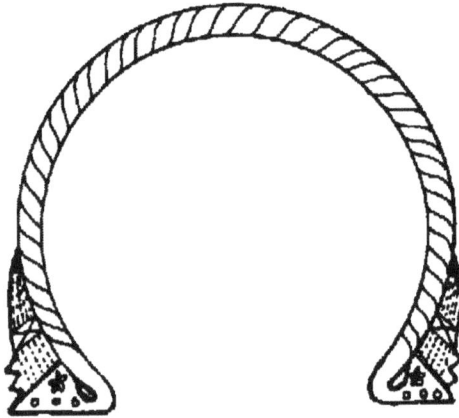

$$A = \text{ᑲA}$$

ᑭA, ᖠA, ᑐA, ᒥA, ᑎᖓᑲA

A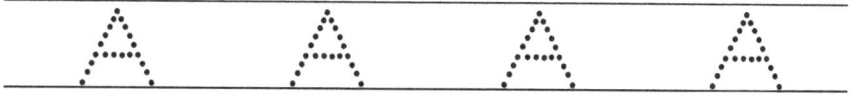

A

A

A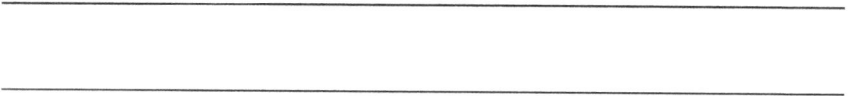

A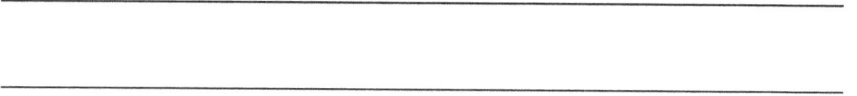

A

ᤜ᤺ᤠ	ᤜᤣᤣ	ᤜᤠᤰᤱᤠ

ᖫ

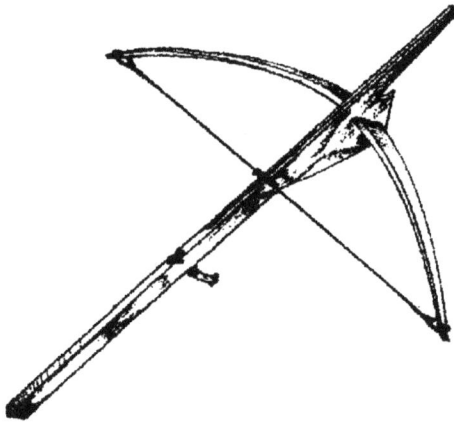

ᖫ = ᗡᖫ

ᑌᖫ, ᗝᖫ, ᗝᖫ, ᐞᖫ, ᑡᖫ

Ħ

Ħ

Ħ

Ħ

Ħ

Ħ

| ᴴⱽᴬ̌ | ᴴⱷⱳ̌ | ᴴᴧ̇ᴿⱨᴣ |

Ч

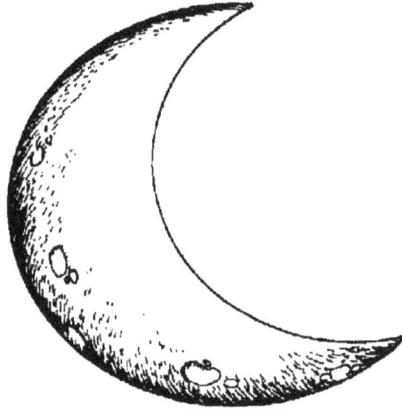

Ч = ᕼЧ

ᑌЧ, ᗯЧ, ᐃЧ, ᑌЧ, ᕼЧ

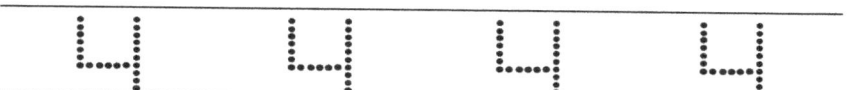

ᤕᤧᤠ	ᤕᤩ	ᤕᤠᤖᤡ

ກ

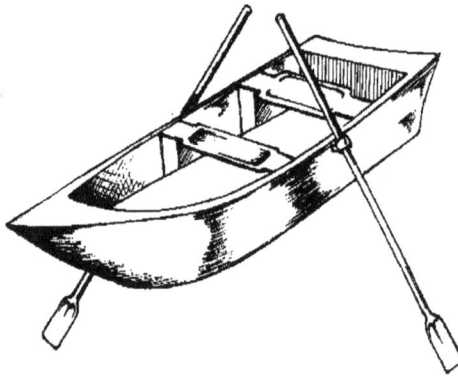

ກ = ເຮືອ

ກິນ, ຈິກ, ກິນເຫຼົ້າ, ກິນເຂົ້າ

ก

น น น น

น น น น

น น น น

ฯฯฯฯ | ฯฯฯฯ | ฯฯฯฯฯ

ມ

ມ = ມ້າ

ວມ, ຍມ, ຕິມ, ບມ, ໜຳມ, ໝມ

Ṷ

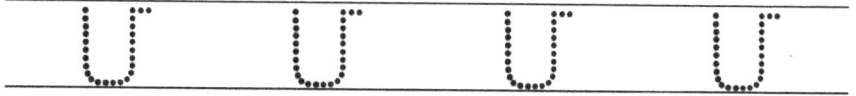

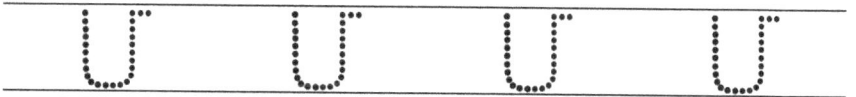

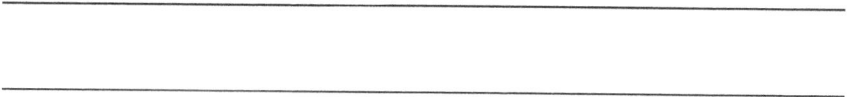

꩟ꩳꩡ	꩟ꩮꩳ	꩟ꩭꩳ꩟

บีก

ᘔ = ᘈᘔ

ᗯᘔ, ᗅᘔ, �, ᘔᘔ, ᗌᘔ, ᘘᘔ

ᤍᤠᤰᤔᤠᤧᤏᤠᤱᤧR ᤕᤧᤴᤔᤢᤱ

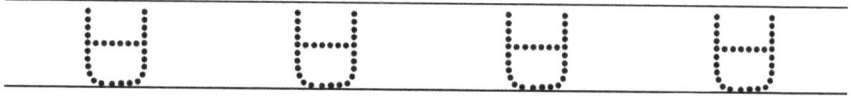

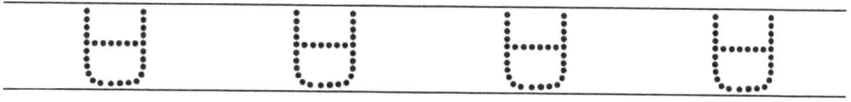

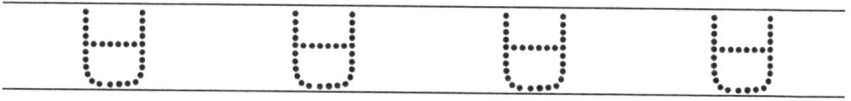

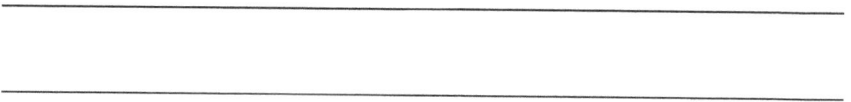

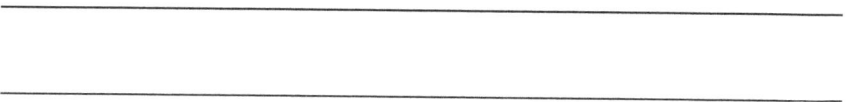

ᤕᤧᤅᤵᤠ	ᤕᤧᤗᤧᤴ	ᤕᤠᤖᤧᤵᤕᤠ

M

M = ШM

ບ̄ແM, ШMແ̆ແ̆ ແ̆, ШMບ̄ໄ̆ ໄ̆∀

[illegible]

M M M M M

M M M M M

M M M M M

M

M

M

[illegible]	[illegible]	[illegible]

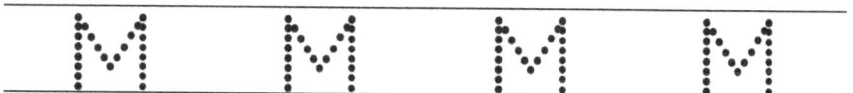

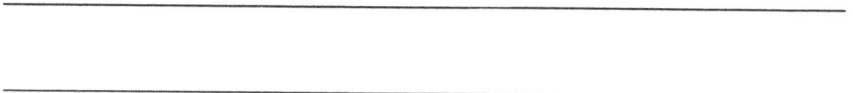

ᑎ

ᑎ = ᯀᑎ

ᗯᑎ, ᯀᑎᗷᯪ, ᗞᗷᗰᯬᯀᑎ

E

E = ᏗE

ᎥE, ᏭE, ᎠE, ᎮE, ᏇE, ᎭE

E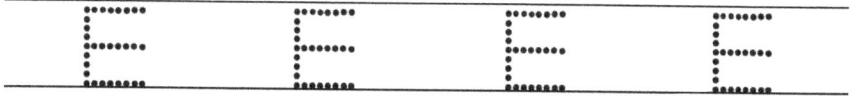

E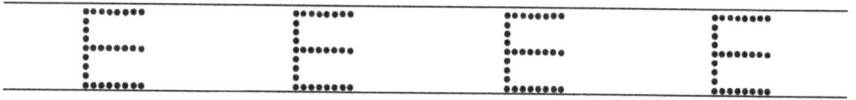

E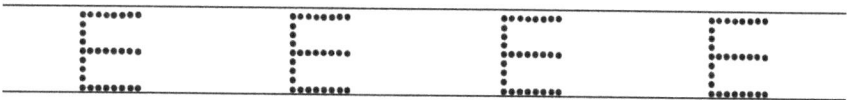

E

E

E

ꞩ ꞏꞏ	ꞩ ꞏꞏꞏ	ꞩ ꞏꞏꞏꞏ

ປ

ປ = ຕໍປ

ພປ, ກິວ໌ ຕໍປ, ຫາຫຶວ໌ ພປ

U U U U U

U U U U U

U U U U U

U

U

U

| ꤢꤛꤢꤨ | ꤗꤢꤪꤥ | ꤗꤢꤟꤛꤢꤛꤢ |

ᮌ = ᮔᮨᮌ

ᮔᮨᮌ, ᮞᮛ ᮔᮨᮌ ᮘᮞ ᮊᮛ ᮏᮛ ᮔᮨᮊ ᮔᮨᮌ

ꖺꕙꕮ	ꖺꕍꖸ	ꖺꕷꖸꖴꕮ

ㅃA ᐱA

●

▼

▬

●●

⏏

ᐱA ㄸR 5 ㅁㅠ

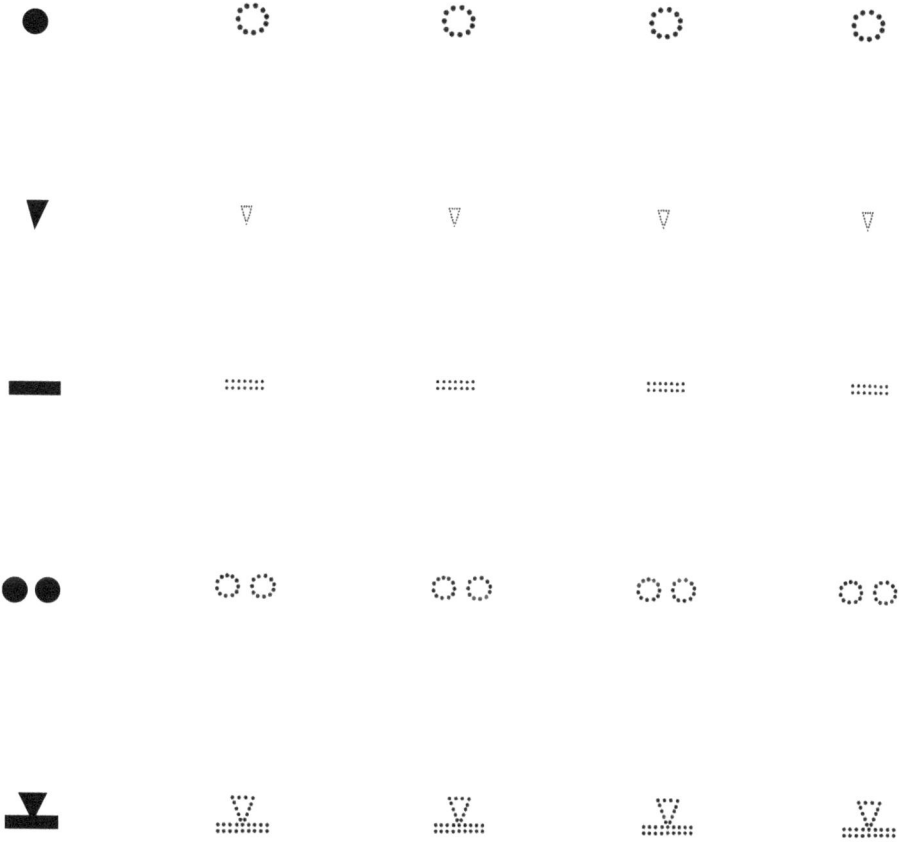

ບົບ ທີ່

ຄຳ ນຳ	ຄຳ ... ນາຍ	... ນາຍ
	_____	_____
	_____	_____
	_____	_____
	_____	_____
	_____	_____
	_____	_____

ບົມ ທີ ໑໖

ພາບ ລາກ	ກິລ ຫາຍ	ຫາກ ລານ ຫາຍ
	_____	_____
	_____	_____
	_____	_____
	_____	_____
	_____	_____
	_____	_____

ᠥᠨᠥ ᠯᠥᠭᠡ	ᠭᠢᠵᠢᠭ ᠪᠠᠶ	ᠪᠠᠪᠠ ᠯᠥᠭᠡ ᠪᠠᠶ
	_____	_____
	_____	_____
	_____	_____
	_____	_____
	_____	_____
	_____	_____

104

ບົບ ທີ ໑໕

ຄຳ ທີ່ ເຫັນ	ຄິດ ຫາຍ	ຫາຫ ເບິ່ງ ຫາຍ
	_____	_____
	_____	_____
	_____	_____
	_____	_____
	_____	_____
	_____	_____

ບົດ ທີ ໑

ຄຳ ນາມ	ກ່ຽວ ບານ	ນາກ ບຫ໌ ບານ
	_____	_____
	_____	_____
	_____	_____
	_____	_____
	_____	_____
	_____	_____

ບົດ ທີ່

ຄຳ ນາມ	ກິລິ ຍາ	ຄຳ ຄຸນ ນາມ
	_____	_____
	_____	_____
	_____	_____
	_____	_____
	_____	_____
	_____	_____

ບົບ ທີ ້ ໌

ຄຳ ນຳ ໃນ	ກ່ວ້ ຫາຍ	ມາກ ໃນ້ ຫາຍ
	_____	_____
	_____	_____
	_____	_____
	_____	_____
	_____	_____
	_____	_____

ບົຍ ຫິ່ວ້

ຮ້ານ ລານ	ຄິນ້ ຫາຍ	ຫາຫ ລນ້ ຫາຍ
	_____	_____
	_____	_____
	_____	_____
	_____	_____

ㆠㅆㄥㆄ

ㄥㆅ ㆁK ㅓR ㆆㅆ

ㄥㆅ ㆁK ㅓR ㆆㅆ........ ㅆㅆ�667ㆆㅎ........ ㅗㆤㆁ ㅓㄥ
ㆠㄱ ㅅK ㆆㅎ ㅓㄥ........ ㄥㆅ ㅗㄥ ㅅㆁ........ ㆆㅎ ㅗㅆ ㄥㆅ ㆤㄥ
ㆤㅈK ㄸㆤ ㅓㆅ ㄸㄴ........ ㆆㄴ ㆤㆁ ㅓ ㆁㅓ ㅓㆅ
ㅓ ㆤㆆ ㅓ ㅓㆅ.......... ㅓ ㆆㆤ ㆠㆤ ㆆㆤ ㆤㆁ

ㅗㆆ ㄥㆅ ㆁK ㆆㄴ........ ㅆㅆ�667ㅓㆁ........ ㆤㄥ ㅅK ㆁㆁ
ㅆㅆ67ㆤ ㄸㆤ ㆠㆅ........ ㆆㅈ ㆤ ㅓㅗ ㅓ ㆆㅗ ㅗ ㅓK
ㅅㆁ ㄸㆤ ㆆㆅ ㆠㆅ........ ㅆㅆ ㆆㆢ ㆆㄴ ㅅㆅ ㅓㆅ
ㆆㆢ ㆆㄴ ㅅㆅ ㅓㄴ........ ㅓ ㆁㆁ ㅓ ㅓK

ㆆㄴ ㆁㆁ ㅓ........ ㆆㄴ ㆤ ㄴㆆ ㆁㆁ ㆁㆁ
ㄥㆅ ㆆㅆ ㄴㆆ......ㆆㆤ ㆤㄴ ㄴㆆ
ㆤ ㆤ ㅓ ㄴㆆ.......ㄸㅓ ㄸㆅ ㄴㆆ
ㄴㄴ ㅓㆆ ㆆㅈ......ㆆㄴ ㆠㆅ ㅗㆤ

ㅂㆁ ㄴㆅ ㆆㄴ ㆤㄴ........ ㄸㅓ ㆆㆅ ㆆR
ㅆㅆ ㄴㆆ ㄴㄴ ㅓㆅ........ ㄴㆆ ㆤㆅ ㆆㆁ ㆁㆁ
ㆆㅆ ㆆㅗ ㅓK............ ㆤR ㆤㆅ ㆤR ㅓㆁ
ㆠㅆ ㆆㆅ ㆆㆆ ㅓㆁ........ ㄴㆆ ㅅK ㆤR ㆠㅓ ㆁㅓ
ㆆㄴ ㆆㆅ ㆠㆆ ㆤㅓ........ ㄴㆆ ㆁㅈ ㄴㆆ ㆆㄴ

110

[Poem in non-Latin constructed script, arranged in two columns with dotted leaders]

ᗑᐊ ᐯᖉ ᐞᛕ ᒍᑫ ᗑᐊ ᐞᛕ ᒥᖉ

ᗷᛕ ᗆᘏ ᗏᑌ ᑕᒍᛌ ᗆᗅᑦᗷᗩᑫᘏ ᒍᑫ ᗪᛌ ᗷᘏ ᗷᗩᑫᗆᛕ ᑭᛌ ᗑᏟ ᗆᗩᗘᏟ ᗏᏟ ᗆᒍ ᗆᑫ ᗷᐞ ᗑᖉᗆᏟ ᗆᖇᗆ ᑭᛌ.

ᗑᗆ ᗑᑫ ᗑᑭᛌ ᑐᗆ ᗆᛕ 75

ᒍᗑᗆ ᐞᛕ ᑫ ᗑᏟ ᒍᐞᑕ

ᗆᛕ ᐯᛕ ᐯᖉ

ᗑᗆ ᐯᖉ ᐞᛕ: ᒍᐞᑕ ᗑᏟ
ᗑᗆ ᐞᛕ ᒥᖉ: ᗑᗆᗆ ᗑᗅ
ᗑᗆ ᗆᛕ ᒍᑕ: ᐞᗅ ᗑᗆ ᗑᏟ
ᗑᗆ ᗷᗆ ᗷᗅ ᒍᗆ: ᗷᑌ ᗑᗅ ᗑᏟ

ᗷᛕ ᗆᘏ ᗏᑌ ᐞᛕ ᗆᛕ ᗆᗷᗆᑫ ᗆᗆ ᗆᏟ ᗑᗩ ᗷᛕ.
ᗆᗆ ᗑᗩ ᗆᖇ ᗆᑌ ᗆᗩ ᒍᗆ.
ᗘᑌ 8/17/2003

113

www.ingramcontent.com/pod-product-compliance
Lightning Source LLC
Chambersburg PA
CBHW081256040426
42452CB00014B/2528